G000141630

DEVON

A portrait in colour

ANDY WILLIAMS
with text by Shân Toyne

Introduction by
Brian Le Messurier

COUNTRYSIDE BOOKS

Other counties in this series include:

BUCKINGHAMSHIRE	HAMPSHIRE
CHESHIRE	SUFFOLK
DORSET	SURREY
ESSEX	SUSSEX

First Published 1994
© Andy Williams 1994

All rights reserved
No reproduction permitted
without the prior permission
of the publishers:

COUNTRYSIDE BOOKS
3 CATHERINE ROAD
NEWBURY, BERKSHIRE

ISBN 1 85306 283 9

Cover design by Mon Mohan
Produced through MRM Associates Ltd., Reading
Typeset by Paragon Typesetters, Clwyd
Printed by Ian Allan Printing Ltd., Addlestone

Contents

INTRODUCTION

Devon is a spacious county, as broad as Cornwall is long, and on three of its four sides it has recognisable physical boundaries – the Bristol Channel, the English Channel and the river Tamar. Only on the east is the boundary line a problem to follow, and there seems little logic for much of its line where it separates Devon from Somerset and Dorset.

As Devon's links with Europe become more frequent and secure, it is of interest to note how similar is its shape to that of France. Each has a dissimilar north and south coast with separate territories to east and west. The analogy can be extended by observing that Lundy is in a similar situation to North Devon as the Channel Islands are to France. I live in that part of Devon which corresponds with the position of Lyon in France so I regard myself as neutral in my attitude to the attractions of this beautiful county.

While I cannot claim it has the diversity of its cross-Channel neighbour, the range of landscape variety within Devon is surprisingly wide, and is a source of constant amazement to American visitors who are used to travelling hundreds of miles through one type of scenery before entering another.

The shape of the county, its relationship with historical enemies (Spain and France), and the course the railway took through the peninsula 150 years ago have influenced our present-day understanding of Devon. I find that while Devonians are quite likely to take a trip into Cornwall, the reverse is not the case. Cornishmen tend to travel through Devon to points east, and not linger here. Likewise, not many North Devonians have an intimate knowledge of the South Hams, as the large chunk of land between Dartmoor and the English Channel is called, and *vice versa*. And the keen walker in the Dartmoor National Park feels the Exmoor National Park is rather tame, while the Exmoor *aficionado* may be slightly worried by Dartmoor's higher, more threatening aspect.

An overview of Devon should also take into account the centres of population, and here there appears to be a curious anachronism. Plymouth, the largest settlement, with a population of about a quarter of a million, is not the county town. This is an accolade held by the more centrally sited but smaller city, Exeter. Plymouth now has a university, but its fringe position *vis-à-vis* the rest of the county means that it is not a centre for the life of Devon, as Exeter can claim. To take just one example, Exeter has a flourishing livestock market – now mostly under cover – and the Devon County Agricultural Show is held nearby.

If we are assembling a balance sheet of advantage and disadvantage, the setting of Plymouth facing the Sound has to be its chief asset. Here is a seascape which thrills all who see it. To stand on the Hoe and look out to sea while exercising the imagination is to relive all those epic voyages which have started or ended here, from the fleet sent out to defeat the Spanish Armada, to the *Mayflower* with the Pilgrim Fathers in 1620, up to the recent task force despatched to the Falklands.

Plymouth is constantly fighting moves to reduce the

Navy, emasculate the dockyard and to correct what it sees as other disadvantages, such as the lack of a decent airport and the fact that the M5 ends just west of Exeter. That a modern dual-carriageway now goes well past Plymouth and into Cornwall is disregarded; on maps this does not show as the mystical blue motorway symbol.

Exeter, on the other hand, has a large airport which supports an (admittedly) infrequent trans-Atlantic service, as well as schedules to the Continent and Ireland, among many other destinations.

Exeter also has its splendid cathedral, and a history going back 2,000 years, and with the presence of County Hall is a true focus for the area. Numerous Devon institutions have their headquarters in the city. It lacks the sea, of course, though it has made the most of its river frontage since 1945, and both north and south coasts can be reached without trouble.

The three towns of Torquay, Paignton and Brixham have coalesced in local government terms to become Torbay, though they retain their own identities to a considerable degree. The fourth largest Devon urban area is Exmouth, the family resort *par excellence*. The two-mile sea front, the longest in Devon and Cornwall, boasts a fine sandy beach. Exmouth is near enough to Exeter to be a dormitory town, and this helps to make the Exeter to Exmouth railway line one of the few flourishing branch lines in the West Country.

Barnstaple in North Devon is a kind of mini county town with its own district hospital, and acts as the pivot for a vast area. Miraculously it retains a railway link with the outside world, and the use of those last two words is not meant disparagingly. When one is in North Devon, one feels slightly detached from the rest of England.

Between Exeter and Barnstaple a wide east-to-west swathe of thinly-populated land runs across Devon, which is no respecter of county boundaries, as it seeps into Cornwall one way and Somerset the other. Within this corridor there are no large towns, and the scene is one of scattered farms and villages in a rural landscape.

If Devon strikes the visitor as a 'cider and cream tea' county this is because much of it is truly rural. But communications with the rest of the world are excellent. InterCity trains speed the traveller from Exeter to Paddington in between two and three hours; coaches take only slightly longer; planes fly to Heathrow and London Docklands airports; ships sail to France and Spain.

One can live in Devon – as I have – for over 50 years, and only scratch its surface. The photographs which follow, together with their extended descriptive captions, give an idea of the beauty and interest of the real Devon.

Brian Le Messurier
Exeter, July 1994

Exeter Cathedral

The cathedral church of St Peter is Exeter's architectural gem, with its two massive Norman towers and majestic proportions. Unlike so many other cathedrals it does not dominate the city skyline except from a few unexpected and glorious vantage points.

There was a minster on the site in Saxon times and the present 'new' building was begun in the early 12th century taking three generations, and more, to complete. It is a monument to the centuries and each successive generation has left an imprint. The illustration shows the great west front which modern paint analysis has shown was once richly coloured with costly pigment. It would surprise the visitors who stroll on the grass of the cathedral green to know that they are walking on a cemetery, with bodies in some places ten deep, which archaeologists date from early Christianity in Exeter.

A fund of history is housed under the soaring, unique, 14th century ribbed vault. The minstrels' gallery displays sculptured medieval instruments, including a citole, shawm and bagpipes, played by angel musicians who from their elevated position hear the fine music of worship, enhanced by the gentlemen and boys of the choir. The strong musical tradition of the cathedral is enhanced by the natural acoustics that make it a joy for those who take part in or listen to the concerts and the choirs of today. Zoological and mythological animals battle between good and evil from the highly carved and richly painted bosses. Some 50 of the oldest surviving English misericord carvings include an elephant and a mermaid sharing the choir stalls with amongst others a weight lifter, a dragon and a centaur.

In the north transept is housed the huge astronomical clock, dated 1480. Behind the dial is a door leading to the clock mechanism and in the little door you will find a hole put there in the early 17th century to enable the cathedral cat to keep mice and rats from chewing the weight lines.

With its 60 foot high wood-carved Bishop's throne, blue-grey Purbeck marble columns, medieval stained glass windows and paintings, and early carved tombs, Exeter's Mother Church is a visual and spiritual feast.

In Cathedral Yard is Mol's Coffee House (*inset*), a timber framed building built in 1596, which became a popular place for gentlemen to meet in the 18th century over the newly introduced drink of coffee.

Exeter Quay and Canal Basin

When the Romans invaded, Exeter was the site of the tribal capital of the Dumnonii and represented the furthest limit of Roman civilisation in the West of England. In AD 50 they founded the frontier town of Isca Dumnoniorum on a hill above a navigable river and a safe distance, but not too far, from the sea. Exeter has remained the capital of the South West ever since and through history has fought with its western, and larger rival, Plymouth, for this privilege. Its ancient history is well chronicled and much of the past can be learned from the fine cathedral library containing the Exon Domesday.

Exeter's long and almost constant relationship with the English Crown provides a fund of stories, amongst them that of Catherine of Aragon staying here for her first night on English soil, on her way to become the first of Henry VIII's ill fated wives. Centuries earlier, Edward the Confessor and his Eleanor spent a Christmas here with the newly installed first Bishop of Exeter, Leofric.

Modern Exeter, which lost so many of its fine Georgian buildings and old churches in the air raids of the Second World War, has been lovingly restored, despite some ugly post-blitz buildings, and almost all architectural styles can be found in the city. The four gateways of the old walled city are marked with plaques, and though not easy to find, are well worth the effort. In searching them out you will come across the oldest municipal building in the country, the Guildhall with its Tudor portico and medieval timber roof; Tuckers' Hall, the hall of the Weavers, Fullers and Shearmen; and the Benedictine foundation of the Priory of St Nicholas, to name but a few historic buildings. Exeter, though, is a modern and thriving city with literally a Golden Heart – the pedestrianised shopping centre.

In the days when the Exe was tidal, the city was a thriving port and following the river southwards from West Gate you will arrive at the grand old 17th century Customs House and well-preserved warehouses on the Quay. One of the most comprehensive collections of working boats in the world, Exeter Maritime Museum opened in 1969 and not only has boats to wonder at in the old warehouses but also afloat in the basin. Examples of all the world's water craft, from dug-out canoes and Welsh coracles to junks and sampans, can be found here, with steam tugs and racing yachts, and the much loved Brunel-designed steam canal dredger *Bertha*.

Sidmouth

Sidmouth, a fashionable watering place of the early Victorians, nestles in one of the most delightful of Devon's bays, between the horns of Salcombe Hill in the east and Peak Hill in the west, right in the centre of Lyme Bay. The narrow, deep valley of the river Sid runs down to the sea, with 500 foot red sandstone cliffs, ending on a long beach of steeply shelving pebbles with a number of fishing boats pulled up at its eastern end.

On the west side of the esplanade are the Chit Rocks where the Dame Partington, immortalised by Sydney Smith, lived. Her cottage was swept away by the big storm of 1824 and when speaking on the House of Lord's rejection of the Reform Bill in 1831 Smith compared them to Dame Partington down at Sidmouth attempting to keep out the sea with a mop. 'She was excellent,' he said, 'at a slop or puddle, but should never have meddled with the tempest.'

The hills dividing the Sid valley from those of the Otter and the Axe shelter the town from the north and east winds and it is not surprising that the aristocratic visitors who 'discovered' Sidmouth long before the end of the 18th century gave it the reputation of the oldest watering place on the Devonshire coast. The little river Sid, just over six and a half miles long, is joined by the delightfully named Snodbrook as it wends its way through the villages that take its name – Sidford and Sidbury. In the town there are narrow streets of little shops behind the esplanade, and a museum full of Victoriana, old photographs and Regency prints.

The Duke and Duchess of Kent, with their baby Victoria, later Queen, spent the winter of 1820 in Woolbrook Glen House (now the Royal Glen Hotel), where the Duke of Kent died of a chill.

Three miles outside the town is Slade Farm, now the headquarters of the internationally known Donkey Sanctuary. This was once the home of Thomazine Browne, whose second husband Sir Norman Lockyer was to initiate in 1912 the building of the observatory that bears his name on Salcombe Hill. After many years of neglect the observatory was refurbished by the National Trust and East Devon Council and reopened in 1989 by Patrick Moore, the well-known astronomer.

Sidmouth is also home to the annual International Folk Festival held at the end of each July bringing throngs of musicians and singers, and their followers, from all over the world.

Topsham

Three miles along the Roman road south of Exeter, nestling on a peninsula between the rivers Exe and Clyst, lies the ancient estuary port of Toppa's Ham. The fortunes of the town, so called when Edward I granted a charter for a market here in 1300, were based on its association with the river. The enterprising Courtenay family blocked the approaches to Exeter at Countess Weir, preventing ships reaching the city and forcing them to unload at Topsham. Vessels returning from exporting serge brought back goods from all over the world, and as ballast, bricks from Amsterdam. Bordering the river the 18th century Dutch-style merchants' houses, illustrated, contain many of these small Dutch bricks.

Topsham was said to be 'the last place the good Lord

made, and He didn't stop to finish it, or we would have had sand not mud'. This mud and silt brought down to the estuary by the river Exe over the years provides the food to attract thousands of wading birds and wildfowl and has made the area one of the foremost wildlife sites in the South West. Here you will see avocets (symbol of the RSPB), bar tailed godwits, oyster catchers and dunlin, cormorant and curlew, and in the winter the long skeins of geese honking down to one of their migratory pit stops on Bowling Green Marshes.

The main road skirts the town and this has probably saved the character and scale of this colourful little place with its individual shops, restaurants, and many old pubs and wine bars. A small ferry will take you across the river by Passage House Inn, where you can walk the few miles along the canal bank to the promontory where the Turf Lock Hotel lies on the west side of the Exe.

Continuing downstream on the east side is Lympstone (*inset*), in a small snug bay flanked by red sandstone cliffs. The early Georgian red brick houses, narrow streets and pretty cottages have great character. Formerly a thriving fishing hamlet, its ships went as far as Greenland and Newfoundland for whale. Now the little harbour, guarded by Darling's Rock, has supplanted the fishing vessels with those of leisure sailors and yachtsmen with, like Topsham, a popular sailing club.

Varying in colour and mood with the tides and the seasons, the striking vista of the gentle Haldon Hills on the skyline watches over the rainbow-coloured spinnakers of the yachts as they race by on the river Exe.

Tiverton

In medieval times Tiverton flourished on the wool trade and was written of as the greatest manufacturing town in the county after Exeter. It was strategically placed just above the fords of the Exe and the Loman, and was said to have had over 50 fulling mills at the beginning of the 18th century, manufacturing woollen worsted cloth. Just as the whole industry was beginning to decline, John Heathcoat, a lacemaker driven from his native Leicester by the Luddites in 1816, transferred his lace factory to Tiverton where it still provides local employment.

The Grand Western Canal at Tiverton meanders some twelve miles through gentle countryside to Holcombe Rogus on the Somerset border. The mania for canals in the 1790s led to many grandiose schemes and the Grand Western was originally to have linked the Bristol and English Channels, thereby avoiding sailing round treacherous Land's End, the scene of so many shipwrecks. The first section to be built was the cheapest and most viable and was started in 1810 and this was eventually the only stretch to survive.

Until the 1920s, limestone was transported from the Canonsleigh quarries but today the canal is a country park and a popular tourist attraction. Though man-made, the canal is an important natural habitat with many species of wetland and woodland birds and an abundance of varied wildflowers and plants.

The towpath provides easy walking through both woods and open countryside. In early summer the pink-flowered hemp agrimony attracts the butterflies and the fragrant white water lily can be seen in many parts of the canal. Roach, pike, carp, perch, tench and bream make for excellent coarse fishing.

If you travel along the Grand Western today, you will find that a derelict, neglected waterway has been rejuvenated. You will pass through Tidcombe, where a Bishop of Exeter refused permission for the canal to be built any closer than 100 yards from his home and therefore there will be a loop in your journey. On you will glide through evocative names such as Manley, Sampford Peverell, Boehill, Ayshford, Ebear, Burlescombe and Great Fossend, to Whipcott Bridge where your journey ends at Lowdwells Lock, the first in a series of locks, lifts and inclined plains that used to take the canal over the edge of Exmoor to Taunton.

Bickleigh Bridge

From its source on the Somerset side of Exmoor, the river Exe runs for some 70 miles through Devonshire, entering the county just south of Dulverton and flowing through the uplands of red marls and sandstone to Tiverton and on until it broadens out below Bickleigh. There are surprisingly few villages in this verdant valley above Exeter owing probably to past risks of flooding. The bridges of the Exe valley are numerous but perhaps the prettiest is the five-arched, narrow bridge, dating from the 16th century, at Bickleigh. It was rebuilt in 1890 after serious flood damage.

The bridge is in a picturesque setting with traditional thatched cottages and inns beside the river. Bickleigh Castle, which is a moated and fortified manor house formerly the home of the Courtenays of Powderham and then of the Carews, is nearby. The river provides the power for the water-wheel and milling machinery at Bickleigh Mill. The mill is a popular craft centre and adjacent is a 19th century farm with shire horses and rare breeds, together with a farm museum showing Devon rural life. By the bridge, the Exe is joined by the Dart (not the famous South Devon one) which flows down from Rackenford on the Tiverton to South Molton road.

St Mary's church is filled with 16th and 17th century monuments to the Carew family. One Bampfylde Moore Carew, son of the rector, led a career of vagabondage and became King of the Gypsies and 'Grand Master of the honourable fraternity of beggars' before returning to Bickleigh to die in 1758.

Instow from Appledore

The small seaside resort of Instow is situated on the joint estuary of North Devon's two major rivers, the Taw and the Torridge. Midway between Barnstaple and Bideford, now more readily accessible with the advent of the North Devon Link Road, the village looks across the little 17th century quay and ferry route to Appledore, from where this picture was taken.

The old Front Road of large private houses, which used to be hidden from the sea by walls and trees, has become the Marine Parade with hotels and holiday apartments. The sands of 'Instow of the Twin Rivers' face the entrance to a sea which at high tide is half a mile wide; the sand is fine and flat with no rocks but plenty of shelter amongst the dunes. There is a ferry across the boat-strewn estuary to Appledore.

There has been salmon fishing in Appledore since the time of the Saxons but in order to conserve fish there is now a reduction in licences and therefore fewer village fishermen, though there is still bass to be caught. The shipyards still turn out ships of considerable size though the yards are almost hidden out of sight up the estuary and you could be forgiven for thinking that Appledore was just a pretty fishing village and holiday area. When Appledore Shipbuilders built their new yard in the late 1960s, Bidna Marsh was the largest covered shipyard in Europe and in the 1970s it was the first nationalised yard in Britain.

In recognition of the service of her seamen and ships against the Spanish Armada, Queen Elizabeth I granted Appledore a free port for all shipping and to this day there are no charges on shipping entering, berthing or mooring in the harbour.

Watermouth Cove

Between Combe Martin and Ilfracombe, sheltered under Widmouth Head, lies the natural harbour of Watermouth.

Boyle and Payne's *Devon Harbours* (pub. Christopher Johnson 1952) tells a fine tale of a 300 ton laden, three masted schooner, the *Polly and Emily* having to take shelter suddenly in this tiny gap in the cliffs. The captain, with a crew of three men and a boy, had to work hard. The halyards were let go and down came the five lightest sails, the flying jib and to'gallant square sail, the main topmast staysail, and the main and mizzen gaff-topsails. As she came nearer the rocks down came more sails; still she ran towards the rocks but suddenly there was a little puff of wind and her three big gaff-sails were filled – and she was in harbour.

The big sails came down and the *Polly and Emily* was able to anchor well up in Watermouth Harbour. Carts arrived on the beach and the crew winched out the cargo of artificial manure. When she was ready to leave for the sea, light southerly airs wafted her out with Hangman and Holdstone Down towering a thousand feet above her masts. No bigger vessel had ever been into this diminutive cove and none so large will come again, under sail and with no engines. Today it is a yacht harbour, a berth in the winter for small sail and motor boats.

There are good cliff walks in both directions and the whole area abounds in picturesque and romantic scenery with sheer cliffs, woody glens and foaming rivers, so very different from the scenes and views of Devon's southern coast.

Running nearby is part of the South West Peninsula Coast Path, the longest footpath in Britain and well charted with acorn-symbolled signposts and sometimes slate or granite stones set in the ground.

Hartland Point

Rising 350 feet from the sea, which can be like a mill pond on one side and boiling on the other, Harty Point, in nautical language, runs out on a turfy isthmus bounded by sheer precipices.

Before the lighthouse was built in 1874 a road had to be cut into the cliff and the initial surveys made offshore in a small boat. The remains of the Point's last victim, the Panamanian *Joanna*, rest on the rocks below, going aground 400 yards from the lighthouse in 1982. This rugged coast that is so very typical of North Devon, with its steep rocky slopes, and scenic cliffs sometimes draped in green, have no land between them and America.

The Hartland peninsula has a long and fascinating history. King Alfred willed it to his elder son Edward; Canute granted it to Gytha on her marriage and after the Norman conquest it was seized by William.

Lundy (Norse for Puffin Island) can be seen eleven miles away. Occupied in prehistoric times and then inhabited by pirates, now the 920 acres are shared by the inhabitants with rabbits, colonies of puffins, and seals but no cars. The only place to land is at the south east end by Rat Island, one of the few remaining habitats of the original black rat now virtually exterminated by the brown rat. Lundy, Britain's first Marine Nature Reserve, is now owned by the National Trust, though financed, administered and maintained by The Landmark Trust, a charity which restores historic buildings and places of natural beauty.

Hartland Quay (*inset*) was a gateway to the world for 300 years, when ships fought the elements to unload. The storms swept the quay away in the 19th century but when it was intact its shape was somewhat like Clovelly with a straight length out to the Life Rock and then a crook eastwards making a closing arm. Tradition has it that the first cargo of guano to arrive in England was landed at Hartland Quay.

Lynmouth

Lying at the foot of cliffs rising sometimes to 1,000 feet, Lynmouth is a cluster of houses and cottages, craft and gift shops, and little tea rooms. Through a beautiful gorge, or cleave, the East Lyn river breaks through to the sea.

In the Memorial Hall you can see photographs of the village as it was before the devastating floods of 1952 when torrential rain on Exmoor brought an estimated 90 million tons of water surging down the valley, destroying nearly 100 houses.

The water-powered cliff railway, the steepest in the world, built in 1890, connects Lynmouth with her larger sister, Lynton, 500 feet up the hill.

At the turn of the century the lifeboat was called to rescue 15 sailors on the full rigged *Forest Hall* in distress at Porlock Bay. In the dark and with a hard wind and ebbing tide, the lifeboat *Louisa* could not be launched and there was only one thing possible to do; every man, woman and boy turned out, together with all the horses that could be found. They pulled the *Louisa* up Countisbury Hill eastwards and over the 1,000 foot Foreland, slipping wooden blocks behind the wheels to prevent a backward run. The complicated descent included digging out hedgerows to give the needed width and even knocking down the corner of a cottage. At six in the morning, drenched with rain and spray, the men of Lynmouth launched their boat, twelve miles from home, and rescued all the crew.

A short distance from Lynton is the famed 'Valley of the Rocks' with strangely bizarre outcrops running parallel to the sea for nearly two miles. Grazing on the bracken slopes are wild but docile goats, found nowhere else on Exmoor. Shelley, Coleridge and Wordsworth are amongst the many who have found this area a romantic source of inspiration.

Where the East Lyn merges with Hoar Oak Water at Watersmeet (*inset*) you find a fairy tale of waterfalls and magnificent oak woods. Owned by the National Trust, an 1830s fishing lodge is now a café where you can sit out on the lawn under the trees.

Ilfracombe

There is a bracing climate in this largest resort in north Devon and wonderful views of the Welsh hills and coastline across the narrow Bristol Channel or, as it was called more romantically in times past, the Severn Sea. Ilfracombe's exceptional seafront sees spring tides rise and fall by as much as 28 feet.

Justly proud of consistently winning awards in the Britain in Bloom competition, the streets are massed with flowers from June to October.

Though most of the town was built after the railway reached the coast in 1847, if you climb Lantern Hill you will find the mainly 15th century chapel of St Nicholas, which looks out over every part of the harbour, kindling thoughts of its long maritime history. Since the Reformation this little building has carried a lantern on its roof and during its 700 years has been firstly a place of pilgrimage, then a home, and even a laundry and a café.

In 1312, 'Ilfard cumme with Brigge warder (Bridgwater) and Barde staple' were ordered to provide three ships to aid the King's service against 'Robert de Brus' and later six ships and 96 mariners from Ilfracombe joined Edward III's fleet of 700 ships to besiege Calais.

To the east is the 447 foot promontory of Hillsborough Hill, crowned by an Iron Age earthwork, from where the main picture was taken. To the west lie Great Hangman and Little Hangman, majestically sheltering one of the longest village streets in England, the one and three-quarter miles of Combe Martin (*inset*). In the fertile combe (Celtic for valley) flows the river Umber, from which umber used to be extracted, and strawberries were grown here by the boatload for the Swansea market. Combe Martin's gentle charm and picturesque scenery are appreciated by one and all.

Exmoor

Exmoor lies within Somerset (the larger part) and Devon. In the east is the cultivated country, stone farmsteads, big beech-hedged fields, and forests. Inland the highest point of the moor, Dunkery Beacon is the start of the uplands that range north-westwards across the park. This high land catches all the Atlantic clouds, with rainfall of

up to 60 inches a year, a gathering ground of many streams and rivers.

The generally soft and undulating contours of Britain's smallest National Park (265 square miles) range from the heights of Hangman above Combe Martin, to the bustling country town of Dulverton. Strikingly empty and largely unexploited, the moor's compact size has great diversity. As a foil to the smooth grass uplands, the steeply cut valleys shelter Exmoor's magnificent shy red deer. South of County Gate, on the A39, are the Oare and Badgworthy Valleys, so much the centre of Doone country that they are actually named as such on Ordnance Survey maps. *Lorna Doone*, Richard Doddridge Blackmore's classic romantic adventure is based on a true bandit family who carried out their nefarious activities here in the 17th century. Henry VIII, possibly because of his own girth together with the needs of his cavalry, ordered the slaughter of all horse sires less than 14 hands but fortunately many native ponies escaped, saved by the remote regions in which they lived. For centuries the high moorlands of Exmoor have provided a natural refuge for herds of small ponies with distinctive mealy coloured muzzles and wiry winter coats. Badgworthy (pronounced 'Badgery') Water is spanned by a pack-horse bridge at the village of Malmsmead, shown here, and on a pleasant and easy walk along the river southwards from the village towards the heart of Exmoor you may see these unmistakable ponies with their light coloured muzzles and colouring round the eyes. They have run wild and bred true longer than any other British breed.

Barnstaple

The Domesday survey records Barnstaple as one of the four boroughs of Devon with a mint and a market; the other three Saxon boroughs were Exeter, Totnes and Lydford. 'Barum' has always been the capital of North Devon; a tree-covered motte (mound) is all that remains of the old castle that used to stand at the meeting points of the Taw estuary and the river Yeo, making a strategic triangle. The river is crossed by a 13th century stone bridge of 16 arches, and although altered over the years, it still shows its medieval origins.

The valleys of the Taw and Torridge form 'Tarka Country', from Henry Williamson's *Tarka the Otter* tale. Trails and walks of great natural beauty are planned carefully to protect the environment.

Two hundred yards downstream is what used to be the town quay, from where five ships sailed to fight the Spanish Armada. A statue of Queen Anne, with gilded crown and mace, surmounts the fine Georgian colonnades of the open portico known as Queen Anne's Walk. Many of the town's 19th century buildings stand out because of the large quantities of buff-yellow 'Marland' bricks, often used with red bricks to make decorated patterns. They were in use until 1918 when they were no longer produced locally.

Fairs and markets have always been an important part of this pleasant town where the cattle market is still held

every Friday and the pubs therefore stay open all day. Behind the Grecian pillars of the Georgian guildhall is the famous traditional and craft Pannier market. Great iron girders support its enormous sloping glass roof. The modern Green Lanes shopping centre is also under cover and nearby are pretty little alleys and flower-filled courtyards. St Anne's chapel, once the grammar school of the Barnstaple-born author of *The Beggar's Opera*, John Gay, is now a museum.

Clovelly

On the coast eleven miles from Bideford is Clovelly, North Devon's most picture-postcard of villages, and one of the pleasantest ways to approach it is along the two and a half mile Hobby Drive; an unmetalled private toll road winding through ancient woodland with magical glimpses of the sea and coastline way below.

Above the village there is a large car park and a charge is made via the Visitors' Centre, in order to enter this privately owned village. Not as much of a trap as it sounds, for this is one way of controlling the thousands of visitors at the height of the season and at the same time contributing to the substantial maintenance of a living village.

Up-a-Long, Down-a-Long, depending on which way you are walking, is the name of the famous cobbled and stepped main street which has changed very little through the years; the 400 foot descent in less than half a mile used to have an open stream but this is now underground, as are all the main services. This unique village is therefore spared overhead wires and poles, though all goods including furniture (and the milk!) are delivered by sledge, for no vehicles are allowed. Tree fuchsias and hydrangeas pack the window boxes of the jumble of whitewashed cottages.

Listed in the Domesday Book as Cloueleia, records show there was a cliffside settlement here in the 13th century where people lived by fishing, especially for herring. Giant sea-beaten boulders make the walled quay which could shelter 60 boats, but now the herring shoals have all but disappeared taking an important industry away.

One of the most influential owners of the village was Christine Hamlyn, a formidable lady who for over 50 years controlled (and they say patrolled) the village, until her death in 1934. She cared for her tenants and restored many of the older cottages, and by forming the Clovelly Estate Company ensured that her beloved village was unspoiled by tourism. She must smile down on the chocolate box scene and the donkeys which used to contribute so much to the commercial success of the village. Despite the many visitors from all over the world, time does seem to have passed Clovelly by.

Bideford Long Bridge

On the east side of the Torridge, where it begins to widen, lies East-the-Water, an area that once housed the greater part of Bideford's prosperous shipyards. Joining it to Charles Kingsley's 'little white town' of Bideford 'is a veritable esquire, bearing arms of its own' (a ship and a bridge proper on a plain field).

Ancestors of the great Elizabethan coloniser, Sir Richard Grenville, built the earliest bridge of oak timber and these timbers were used as scaffolding for the first stone bridge constructed in the 15th century. Nearly 680 feet long with 24 irregular pointed arches, this listed Ancient Monument has a venerable personality.

A new bridge was built downstream in 1987 to carry the A39 North Devon Link Road and this to many is equally an engineering feat and design of its time, which also keeps the town free from heavy traffic.

Travelling from the famous old Long Bridge towards the tree-lined quay, you see it busy with every type of boat including Lundy's passenger and supply ship which sails from here and from Ilfracombe. The town itself mounts in tiers on the hillside with lines of predominantly Victorian architecture, though wide Bridgeland Street has splendid 17th century merchants' houses. Bideford too has its Pannier market hall together with a modernised and pedestrianised shopping area. The river front is attractively wide and almost has the air of a French riverside town.

North of Bideford the Atlantic rollers of Westward Ho break on to two miles of golden sand. The amazing Pebble Ridge, 50 feet wide and 20 feet high, acts as a barrier between the sea and Northam Burrows Country Park.

Torquay

Between the two hills of the Vane and Waldon lies Torquay harbour, tucked into the northern end of the wide sweep of Tor Bay.

A focal point of Torquay, the main resort of the English Riviera, the little man-made inner harbour, offers pleasure cruises and fishing trips and on a balmy day holidaymakers escape the congestion of the harbour pavements and shopping centres to sail out into the bay. In 1850 the town was known as 'the Montpelier of England' and the 'Queen of Watering Places'. From the sea you look back at the white villas, guest houses and hotels dotting the wooded contours, fringed at their base with palm trees. The twelve mile sweeping arc of the bay, from Berry Head in the south to Hope's Nose in the north, offers large and safe anchorage and on all but the windiest of days this area is dotted with water sports enthusiasts and white sails. The quaintly named Daddy Hole Plain to the east of the harbour has superb views out over the bay and down to the green-grassed top of Thatcher Rock, lying south of Hope's Nose and the Coastguard lookout.

The socio-economic changes of the last generation or two have changed Torquay's genteel image, and though her equable climate attracts winter visitors and the retired, the summer tourists still flock here. There is plenty of entertainment and safe bathing from the fine red sandy beaches and, after exploring the town, there is a wealth of quiet countryside to explore once off the main road.

Totnes

The sea and the moor are both easily accessible from the historic town of Totnes, which lies some seven miles inland at the highest tidal point on the river Dart. From the highest point in the town, the battlements of the ruined Norman castle command a fine view of the town, surrounding hills and the valley below. From the castle runs the High Street where grey slated fronts are supported by pillars, some granite, some wood and some iron, forming a covered way underneath. Like Dartmouth, Totnes has a 'Butterwalk', a name derived from the days of open markets when butter and cheese had to be kept in the shade.

Halfway down the hill, where High Street joins Fore Street, a picturesque castellated arch bridges the popular shopping thoroughfare. One of three medieval entrances to the Old Town, East Gate was destroyed by fire in 1990 but has now been restored. It is believed though to have been restored once before in 1600. Through the arch a small path follows the Old Town walls to the medieval Guildhall, built on the foundations of the refectory of Totnes Priory in 1553.

Rebuilt by Charles Fowler, the Devon-born architect, in 1828, the three segmental spans of Totnes town bridge belong to a period of solid stone bridge-building. This replaced a much older seven-arched structure on which was a small chapel dedicated to St Edmund. The quayside's old warehouses have been well converted into houses, shops and cafés.

The tranquil scene taken from the bridge (*inset*) shows some of the warehouses which store the timber that is still brought up-river from Finland and Sweden.

Brixham

Brixham huddles up the hill of the south east corner of a low lying peninsula, which forms a neck a mile and a half wide between Galmpton Creek on the Dart and Broadsands on Tor Bay.

Both a busy commercial harbour and a popular holiday resort, here on the southernmost extremity of the bay could be found the last of the great heroic sailing fleets, the brown-sailed two-masted Brixham trawlers. Nowadays you will see a replica of Drake's *Golden Hind*, slightly out of place with the fishing vessels and pleasure boats. William of Orange landed

here on a high spring tide in 1688 to lay claim to the throne of James II and the spot is marked by a red granite obelisk.

Still a colourful and attractive port, Brixham's fishermen's cottages are packed tightly on the surrounding hills. A former vicar of the town, the Rev H F Lyte, wrote some familiar hymns, including *Abide with me*.

The old harbour originally stretched half a mile inland, giving complete shelter, and the central part of Brixham is built over this harbour. It was not until 1916 when the 3,000 foot outer breakwater was completed, taking 70 years to build, that it became a really safe anchorage.

The Brixham trawlers opened up the North Sea fisheries and it was a local man who claimed to have found the once prolific source of the Silver Pits on Dogger Bank. Nowadays Brixham probably lands as many visitors as fish – but it is the very atmosphere of the port that brings the visitors.

A mile north east of Brixham, Berry Head has a tiny twelve foot high lighthouse standing on a 200 foot cliff. Many cliff-nesting seabirds, particularly kittiwakes and fulmars, can be seen soaring around the limestone rocks. Berry Head Country Park includes the huge fort built to guard against possible Napoleonic invasion.

Challaborough

Warmed by the Gulf Stream, this area of the South Hams is on a promontory jutting out into the English Channel, and is reached by turning off the Plymouth to Kingsbridge road and then on through Bigbury. Fairly inaccessible and perhaps because of this, relatively unspoilt, the rolling misshapen farmland is dissected with hedgebanks that are devoid of trees near the coast. This area has a network of tiny narrow lanes, some so little used they have tufts of grass growing in the middle, and with new policies on the uses of pesticides, there is a visual and fragrant feast of wild flowers on the high banks. To some people these glorious green tunnels of sunken lanes are oppressive for you can rarely see over the top; to others they are almost the personification of Devon.

Throughout the centuries farming has been one of the greatest influences on the landscape, and the economy, of Devon. Though sheep and arable farming are the traditional agriculture, this was once one of the biggest cider producing areas. Sadly, in Devon, over 6,000 acres of orchards have gone since 1905 but in the last few years there has been a resurgence of interest in restoring this important feature of the landscape. Thanks to an initiative by Devon County Council and its partners, in 1993 over 2,000 traditional Devon varieties of orchard fruits, cider apples, dessert or culinary apples, pears, plums and cherries have been planted in the County.

Nearly 80% of Devon is used for agriculture and, with its traditional patterns of small fields, copses and hedgerows, it has miraculously managed to avoid the prairies of eastern England. A thriving farming industry is vital to the livelihood of a countryside rich in plant and animal life and also helps to ensure that Devon's other important green industry, tourism, is upheld.

Hope Cove

The 15 mile stretch of gently rolling countryside between Kingsbridge and Plymouth contains three little rivers, the Yealm, the Erme and the Avon. These have quite sizeable estuaries by the time they reach the sea so the coast road was made three miles or so inland and has helped to keep this a pleasantly small and remarkably undeveloped part of the South Hams coast.

From Bolt Head to Bolt Tail stretch five miles of 400 foot cliffs, and sheltering under Bolt Tail is the village of Hope Cove with long associations of smuggling and fishing. Outer Hope and Inner Hope are joined by a new road built after the old one had fallen into the sea, but a walk across the sands, or along the cliff paths, is a wonderful alternative.

One of the earliest works in English literature was a poem about the sea. *The Seafarer* was copied, maybe from a story handed down by word of mouth, or written down, into the Exeter Book, that is a collection of Anglo-Saxon writing dating from the year AD 904. There have been many translations and interpretations of this dramatic poem over the centuries. The Exeter Book was given to the Cathedral in Exeter in the 11th century by Bishop Leofric, and it is well treasured. The poem illustrates so well what must have been the feelings of the Devon fishermen and intrepid explorers. Richard Hamer (in *A Choice of Anglo-Saxon Verse*) translates the richness this way:

'And yet the heart's desires
Incite me now that I myself should go
On towering seas, among the salt waves' play;
And constantly the heartfelt wishes urge
The spirit to venture, that I should go forth
To see the lands of strangers far away.'

Teignmouth

A quirk of economic history has left the mouth of the four mile long Teign estuary with flourishing docks, despite its shallow and difficult entrance and strong tidal currents. The thriving trade in ball clay has kept the tucked away port busy, though the last shipyard closed in 1968. From here Dartmoor granite was shipped to build London Bridge (now in Arizona). The opening of a bridge across the estuary, linking Teignmouth and Shaldon in 1827 brought improved communications, and tourists, to the towns.

Towards the end of the 18th century general lawlessness, generated perhaps by privateering, was rife especially during the years of the American War of Independence. A splendidly patriotic, and greedy, advertisement appeared in the town at that date: 'A new advantageous Plan of Privateering, For a Six Months Cruize. All Gentlemen Seamen and Able Landmen who delight in the Music of Great Guns and distressing the Enemies of Great Britain now have a fine opportunity of making their Fortunes by entering on Board the *Dragon* Privateer... now ready to be launch'd in the Harbour of Teignmouth... Apply Capt Joseph Drew at Stokeintinhead... or Mr Manning, Sailmaker, Teignmouth. NB The Cutter will sail from Teignmouth by the last of March for Guernsey to take in her Stores and proceed on her Cruise against the Enemy. Any Person capable of beating a Drum, or blowing a French horn, shall have great encouragement.'

The photograph opposite looks across the mud flats, known as The Salty, to The Ness at Shaldon. A landmark at the entrance to the estuary, The Ness is a red sandstone tree-covered headland with a long smugglers' tunnel leading to a sheltered tiny beach.

In summer a black and white passenger ferry operates from Teignmouth harbour beach across to the deep red sand and pebble beach of Shaldon (*inset*) where you can sit in a riverside beer garden with marvellous views across to Teignmouth.

The Parson and the Clerk

Midway between Dawlish and Teignmouth are the oddly-shaped rocks called the Parson and the Clerk. Legend has it that a clergyman and his clerk were led by the Devil round the headland and were caught by the tide and turned to stone. The horse on which the poor parson was riding was changed into the Horse Rock.

One of the railway tunnels threading through the craggy red cliffs of Brunel's line, which follows the Exe Estuary and coast to Newton Abbot is, needless to say, called Parson's tunnel. Rising vertically from the sea, great chunks of the red cliffs often collapse during winter storms.

In their time, Keats, Jane Austen and Charles Dickens were all enamoured of this once genteel resort of Dawlish. The railway hides the sea from the municipal flowered lawns decorating the sides of Dawlish Water running through the centre of the town. Ducks and moorhens, and the famous Dawlish black swans, abound in this stepped centrepiece of water running down to the seafront. There is a fine Victorian ornamental station just where the trains cross the seafront on a granite viaduct. Dawlish beach is over a mile long and extends beyond on a sandy spit to the mouth of the Exe, known as The Warren. Beyond the caravan parks and holiday centres are the wild sand dunes of a 500 acre Nature Reserve with many kinds of birds and over 400 species of plantlife including the only site of the sand or warren crocus on mainland Britain. It is an area that has everything from bucket and spade, fish and chip holidays to the wild marram grass and the almost overpowering sweet-smelling sand lupins, and more often than not in high summer, the skylark overhead.

The Dart at Dartmouth

If you enter this most romantic of Devon's rivers from the sea, you are reminded of Dartmouth's sometimes turbulent past by the castles guarding either side of the estuary. The very site of Dartmouth has meant it has had a long and distinguished military and naval history. The Romans, Richard Coeur de Lion, the French, the Royalists and the Roundheads, and in this century the Germans, have all contributed to its past. The encircling hills have protected the town and harbour from the worst of the elements, and sometimes from the invaders.

There is some fine architecture from the quayside right up the steep-sided valley, including terraces of 17th century houses and Georgian inns. The lower part of the town, including Fosse Street and the market place, is built on reclaimed land. The Cherub, a glorious half-timbered pub, circa 1380, is probably Dartmouth's oldest remaining building.

The deep-water harbour has always encouraged those with a love of the sea, and what could be a more fitting site for the training of young naval officers than Britannia Royal Naval College? This most prestigious and world famous naval establishment sits at the far end of the town on the hill above the higher, or Dartmouth, ferry.

Held annually at the end of August is the Royal Regatta, Royal for Queen Victoria attended in 1856. Spectacular firework displays, the customary Royal Navy 'Guard ship' firing her salute, and the RAF's

Red Arrows appearing apparently from nowhere, delight the crowds on their boats or sitting on the surrounding hills, in this magnificent natural amphitheatre.

The lower Kingswear ferry (*inset*) takes cars across to the eastern shore of the Dart. Smaller than Dartmouth, although an earlier settlement, Kingswear is dominated by its railway station, from where the steam trains run along the river bank for two miles before climbing up and through the ridge dividing the Dart Valley from Torbay.

50

Cockington Village

Midway between Paignton and Torquay, and historically one of the ancient parishes of Torquay, snuggles Cockington village. Situated at the bottom of a deep and wooded valley, immaculate pinkwashed cob cottages, topped by thatch, surround the 14th century forge in this carefully preserved 'olde worlde' atmosphere. With horse and trap taking visitors along the winding leafy lanes, this must be one of the most photographed villages in Devon.

The saying goes that a cob wall is like a baby; it must have a dry hat and a dry bottom. Provided it has a hat of thatch and a bottom of stone it will stay warm in winter and cool in summer and survive the centuries. The beauty of so many small Devon villages is owed to these stout cob walls with their haphazard shapes and great individuality. The county is rich in cob, and renewed interest in using natural and traditional materials is producing a cottage industry. A distinctive modern building in the village is the Drum Inn, completed in 1934 and designed by Sir Edwin Lutyens.

Follow the windy lanes down to the Tor Bay coast road, and south past the deep red cliffs of Hollicombe and then Preston Sands, to Paignton. This is a traditional British seaside town, but with a modernised harbour and a wide esplanade and a pier.

Oldway Manor (*inset*) was started in 1874 for Isaac Singer, the sewing machine magnate, and has been called 'The Little Versailles', or as its owner originally planned, 'The Wigwam'. Renamed 'Oldway' by Singer's fourth child, Paris, the 115 roomed mansion has had a chequered life. A family home, a country club, a First World War American hospital and a training wing for the RAF, now the Italianate marble staircase, ceiling frescoes and mirrored gallery house the local council offices, including the Register Office.

Dartington

North of Totnes, centred on a promontory between the A384 and the river Dart, is Dartington House or Hall. It was the seat of a Barony in Domesday, was passed to Richard II who gave it to his half brother, the Duke of Exeter, and in the early 16th century it passed to the Champernowne family.

When bought by Leonard and Dorothy Elmhirst in 1925 it had fallen into rack and ruin. The original buildings consisted of two quadrangles, connected to each other by the hall, the kitchen and the buttery, together with other 'appendages', nearly an acre all told. The creatively restored gardens and buildings became an experiment in the reconstruction of rural life. Responsible for so many innovative ideas, the Elmhirsts' philosophy was for economic development but with a viable and satisfying quality of life; the internationally renowned Dartington String Quartet,

the Dartington Sawmills, and the Dartington Glass factory in North Devon, amongst other projects, were all the result of their inspiration.

The Great Hall with its 50 feet oak frame roof is a joy to behold whether it be to listen to a worthy lecture, a Shakespeare play or a concert that might be part of a glorious annual Dartington Summer School of Music recital. The woven banners hanging in the hall reflect the Elmhirst vision of Dartington; farming, forestry, gardens, masonry, education, and the arts.

Cobbled paths lead through immaculate lawns to the great green amphitheatre of the Tiltyard and a Henry Moore statue reclines under the chestnut trees. In spring carpets of crocus spread out beneath the fine old trees, with the parkland reaching down to the banks of the Dart.

Powderham Castle

More of a fortified manor house than a true castle, Powderham has belonged to the Courtenay family, the Earls of Devon, for more than 500 years. It is far older than would be thought by its present appearance, the oldest part dating from between 1390 and 1420, but it

has been altered and extended, mostly between the 18th and 19th centuries, so that the general effect is of a later date.

The castle is just off the A379 Exeter to Dawlish road, set in an oak-filled deer park on the banks of the river Exe. In the 18th century the river almost reached the east walls. Open to the public part of the year (check with the administrator), it contains some fine interiors, furniture and china. There are paintings by Holbein, Sir Joshua Reynolds, Kneller and Cosway amongst others. A particularly fetching family group by Peters, shows the 2nd Viscount Courtenay and his somewhat exhausted looking wife with eleven daughters and one son, and there were two more daughters yet to come when this was painted!

At the end of the 18th century James Wyatt designed the fine blue and white painted Music Room where the gilt furniture bears the Courtenay family crest, a dolphin.

The shore of the estuary on this western bank of the Exe is dominated by the former Great Western Railway hugging the shore. A prominent feature of Starcross, a mile downriver, is Isambard Kingdom Brunel's red sandstone pumping station. This atmospheric system, based on compressed air in a pipe between the tracks, was a disaster because the action of the water with iron on the important leather valves made them disintegrate. Legend has it that the system was also susceptible to rats eating the leather!

Hatherleigh

The livestock market on Tuesdays is the business and social highspot of the week in Hatherleigh, a characterful mid-Devon town. Covered country market stalls are joined by an area for poultry, small animals and local produce, besides the main sheep and cattle auctions. The Saxons gave the name of 'Hawthorn glade' to the settlement that grew with rivers on three sides, the Lew, the Torridge and the Oakment.

Across the central square is the 15th century church of St John the Baptist, where in the January storms of 1990 the single spire crashed down through the nave – now lovingly restored. Pure drinking water, which runs underground from Hatherleigh Moor, is to be found at Buddle spring in the High Street. It never dries up and water is collected from it daily. For refreshments of another kind, visit the George Hotel, which may have been the courthouse of the Abbots of Tavistock. Built around a courtyard that once served as stables, the George used to be the principal coaching stop between Bideford and Plymouth or Exeter. Cottage industries thrive, with traditional ales (the Tally Ho has its own brewery) and honey and hand-made chocolates.

The 430 acres of Hatherleigh Moor to the east side of the town were given to the inhabitants in the 14th century, probably by a Tavistock abbot, for cutting gorse for fuel and for grazing cattle. These rights continue to this day and the householders are known as 'pot boilers'. From the Hatherleigh Monument (*inset*) you can see Yes Tor, the highest (2,030 feet) tor on Dartmoor.

Some ten miles from Hatherleigh, just south of Torrington is the Royal Horticultural Society's gardens at Rosemoor, a must, especially when the 2,000 roses in 200 varieties are in bloom.

Castle Drogo

Would that one could build a castle now, especially on a site like this, with panoramic views across the valley of the river Teign. Julius Drewe was only 33 years old when he had made enough money from his founding of the 'Home and Colonial Stores' that he was able to retire and set himself up as a country gentleman. The 'e' had been added to the family name of Drew in 1910 following Julius's enthusiastic research into his ancestry and the connection with Drogo de Teign, from whom the parish of Drewsteignton had been named.

A terrific tale of enterprise was unfolded when in 1910 Julius Drewe commissioned one of the great 20th century architects Sir Edwin Lutyens, to build him an ancestral

home, a grandiose castle. Constructed entirely of granite, Lutyens' masterpiece is the last great country home to have been built from new in England. From the river, hundreds of feet below, the great walls and battlements tower upwards in a solid, mullion-windowed, almost overwhelming, mass of hard granite.

Although the original plans (and there even exist sketches drawn by Lutyens on notepaper belonging to the Royal Clarence Hotel, Exeter, while he was staying there) were eventually scaled down, Julius Drewe was rightly well pleased with his Drogo. His attention to detail was such that the size of the gravel and the forecourt were determined by the turning circle of his Silver Ghost Rolls Royce. It was his grandson and great grandson who gave their home and its 600 acres, including the medieval deer park (a Site of Special Scientific Interest), the huge circular croquet lawn and the magnificent geometrical yew-hedged gardens, to the National Trust in 1974.

The village of Drewsteignton stands on a ridge 700 feet above the river Teign. East of Drogo, the village is built round a central square of thatched and cream-painted cottages where The Drewe Arms and the church vie for position. Below the village is the hump-backed ancient monument of Fingle Bridge. In the densely wooded slopes of the Teign Gorge where a level riverside path runs through a glorious wildlife habitat, you may see kingfishers, wagtails, buzzards and fallow deer, and even the occasional otter. Wild daffodils and bluebells, in their special seasons, carpet the woodland on this delightful walk to Steps Bridge.

Dartmoor – Combestone Tor

Dartmoor covers an area of 365 square miles and rises to over 2,000 feet, a backbone to the South West Peninsula. This last great southern wilderness, an old volcanic region, has been a National Park since 1951.

The A38 and A30 define this granite area which was called the 'Forest of Dartmoor' when Henry III first recorded its boundaries.

Over 250 million years ago the molten magma beneath the earth's crust cooled deep underground and solidified. Over millions of years, the covering of sedimentary rock was eroded exposing the raw granite, which natural forces have continued to sculpt and shape into numerous and varied tors. If you look closely at these solid grey masses you can see the rough flecks of brown and white mica glisten, the quartz crystal and, occasionally, the large pink or white feldspar.

The higher and wilder moorland is divided in two by the B3357 and B3212 roads and the majority of tors are around, and visible from, the two high moor roads. On a loop road south towards Huccaby and Hexworthy, complete with its own carpark, is the easily accessible Combestone (pronounced Cumston) Tor, illustrated here with a view to Dartmeet to the north.

Past the tor and downhill a few feet is a man-made Dartmoor leat, originally cut to take water from the O Brook (possibly one of the shortest names in the country) stream to the village of Holne and further on to the Buckfastleigh woollen mills.

Tamar Bridges

The river Tamar forms the dividing line between Devon and Cornwall for most of its entire length and at Cotehele, on the west bank before you reach the Tamar bridges, is *The Shamrock*, the only surviving Tamar barge, a two-masted, 57 feet, cargo boat. Once a common sight on this old trading route, it was still plying its trade until 1970.

At the confluence of the Ham Brook and the Tamar, large mud-flats formed which were called Ham ooze, or mud, from which possibly came the mysterious name of The Hamoaze.

Saltash is a suburb of Plymouth on the Cornish side of the Tamar and you can sit outside one of the splendid pubs at the water's edge and look up at the two massive bridges. Built 100 feet high to allow clearance for shipping, the railway bridge was an astonishing feat of engineering for its time. Great tubular arches were floated into position, with piers built under the jacked-up arches. The central pier sinks 80 feet below highwater and in 1857 huge crowds watched Isambard Kingdom Brunel supervise the first great truss being put into position. Second only in grandeur to his Clifton Suspension Bridge, Brunel's Royal Albert Railway Bridge was opened by the Prince Consort in 1859.

As there was no government money available, the Tamar road bridge was built by Cornwall County Council and Plymouth as a toll bridge and Queen Elizabeth the Queen Mother opened this in 1959, almost 100 years to the day after Prince Albert had opened the railway bridge.

A memorial statue (*inset*) to Plymouth's great pirate admiral, Sir Francis Drake, surveys the maritime scene. Plymouth's patronage, in the 16th century, of Drake and Hawkins, helped establish the city's supremacy as a port. Sailing from here Drake not only defeated the Spanish Armada but in his *Golden Hind* successfully circumnavigated the world in 1577.

Plymouth

'So much of the history of Plymouth belongs to the history of England as a whole ... Plymouth has given its name to some 40 Plymouths all over the English speaking world. What greater testimony is needed to the affection that it has inspired for the past 400 years? It is the mother of all Plymouths everywhere.' (W G Hoskins, *Devon*)

Strategically placed guarding the western approaches to the Channel, between the estuaries of the Tamar and the Plym, Plymouth Sound has one of the finest deep anchorages in Europe, with a massive breakwater protecting it from the prevailing south-westerly winds.

Now the largest conurbation in the South West, an amalgamation of the three towns of Devonport, Stonehouse and Plymouth, it was virtually flattened by air raids during the Second World War. Post-war planners arranged the new commercial centre of the city in the formality of a grid, making it a shopper's delight with a large pedestrianised precinct, flower-filled walkways and colourful mosaics (*inset*). The ceramic murals, in the Armada Way subway, were inspired by the Bayeaux tapestry and designed by Edward Pond. They trace the historic background of the Hoe – starting with Henry VIII and finishing with the Falklands campaign. The city's economy, in the past so dependent on the sea, has diversified with the growth of manufacturing, service and high tec industries but is still very dependent on the dockyards

and defence-related industries.

Sheep and cattle used to graze on the Hoe, the ridge separating the harbour from the city centre, and the red and white striped Smeaton's tower sits strangely proud out of water on this greensward, through history always a pleasant open space for Plymothians. The tower is the third Eddystone lighthouse and was moved here in 1882 when the sea began to undermine it. On a clear day its successor can be seen flashing twice every ten seconds as it marks the entrance to the Sound. In the background of this picture are the fortifications of the Royal Citadel, built in 1666.

Postbridge – Clapper Bridge

In the heart of Dartmoor, the little hamlet of Postbridge has a population of just over 100 people. The toll road from Moretonhampstead to Tavistock was built in the late 18th century, bypassing the old bridge by yards. The 14th century clapper bridge pictured is one of the finest to cross the East Dart river. Great 15 foot by 7 foot granite slabs sit on four piers of granite, kept in position by their own sheer weight.

Amidst a moorland scene of windswept grass and gorse, Postbridge is a popular starting point for Cranmere Pool and its letter box hunters. Because of its situation, and size, this pre-Roman river crossing is possibly the most famous clapper bridge in the world.

Lady Sylvia Sayer, surely one of the only conservationists to have had her name appear in a daily newspaper crossword clue, has inherited from her grandfather Robert Burnard, and father Charles, a deep and protective love affair with 'The Moor'. The Burnard photographs, published between 1890 and 1894 are a remarkable record; they describe Postbridge as 'The Metropolis of the Moor' with at least 14 'pounds' (see Prehistoric Dartmoor) in an area of a square mile.

The variety of wildlife in the different areas of Dartmoor is amazing. You can hear the skylark singing high above the open moorland, and the circling buzzards in the valleys. The upland bog system traps moisture in its deep covering of peat and provides the perfect habitat for wetland plants. White tufts of waving cotton, and purple moor grass flourish in these areas, the only West Country breeding places for golden plover and dunlin.

The once much more widespread heather is the plant on which so much wildlife of the moor depends. A shy moorland blackbird with a white bib, the ring ouzel, can be found in the heather-clad gullies.

Widecombe-in-the-Moor

Tom Pearse, Tom Pearse, and your old grey mare, what have you tried to do to Widecombe-in-the-Moor? With Hameldown ridge on one side and Honeybag, Chinkwell and Bell Tors on the other, this charming village sitting high in the Webbern valley of rugged moorland, deserves to be known for so much more than its popular Devon song. Widecombe Fair, known to have been held in 1850, is still held on the second Tuesday of September and draws huge numbers

of visitors. The 'grey mare' which according to song sickened and died after her epic journey carrying seven riders to Widecombe, is supposed to haunt the route still, and is an attraction of Fair day complete with an authentically costumed Uncle Tom Cobleigh.

The 120 foot tower of the grand St Pancras church dominates the centre of the village and is rightly referred to as the Cathedral of the Moor, for although 14th century it was enlarged thanks to the wealth of the local tinners. In 1638 a thunderstorm killed four of the congregation and in the church tower it is remembered, 'some had skin all over skorcht, yet no harm in the cleaths'.

Small ponies were inhabiting the savage tors and dangerous bogs of Dartmoor as long ago as 1012. They were used between the 12th and 15th centuries for carrying tin, peat and wool off the moors and later for farm work. Though the ponies have since run free, they all have owners and are rounded up at the drift each year. The demand for small pit ponies in the 19th and 20th centuries led to the introduction of Shetland stallions and this cross still persists, though Dartmoors are bred on many studs and recognised worldwide as the best possible riding pony for small children.

Wheal Betsy and Industrial Dartmoor

Wheal Betsy is one of the most dramatic and romantic remains of the mining industry, on a lonely stretch of the western Moor called Black Down, north of Mary Tavy. Its tall chimney is conspicuous from the A386 to Okehampton. The history is shown on a plaque: 'This ancient silver-lead mine was re-opened in 1806 and worked successfully for the next seventy years. The mine was worked by water power until 1868 when this building was erected to house a Cornish beam pumping engine. Until its closure in 1877 all pumping, winding and crushing of ore was carried out by steam power. In 1967 the ruined engine house and stack were acquired and made safe by the National Trust as a memorial to the mining industry of Dartmoor'.

Not everyone thinks of Devon as having such a rich and varied industrial past. The list of materials mined and quarried, on the Moor alone, is endless but mention must be made of a few.

Granite has been quarried at Blackingstone, Haytor, Merrivale and Walkhampton, and the Tavistock area produced the green Hurdwick ash stone.

Golden Dagger mine near Postbridge was crushing ore until 1879 and a tin and copper mine called Little Duke, near Buckland Monachorum, was still being re-worked for arsenic early in this century.

A soft white mineral occurring in granite, barytes, used amongst other things for producing hydrogen peroxide, was mined at Bridford near Christow on the eastern boundary of the Moor.

Meldon Quarry, off the A30 beyond Okehampton is where you might expect granite to be quarried but instead hornfels rock is excavated and processed. When diffused into a solid state to become glassy, it has a quality ideal for ballast which is used under the steel rails of the railways.

Prehistoric Dartmoor

As a building stone, the durability of granite knows no bounds and perhaps this is why there are several thousand prehistoric remains on Dartmoor. The perimeter wall of one of the best known archaeological sites is clearly visible at Grimspound, which is north of Widecombe and three miles west of Manaton.

Covering a four acre site, the dry unhewn stone circle is on the western slope of Hameldown Tor. Inside this 'pound' are the remains of 24 hut circles, half of which showed signs of human habitation in the form of hearths and cooking holes. These are the ruins of walls, dwelling houses and storage and cattle sheds. The huts at Grimspound are slightly smaller than average, between 15 and 17 feet, although they do vary. Where the doorways are wide they were probably byres or store houses and the entrances usually face south west. This would mean the inhabitants had to face the Atlantic rains but would be protected from the north-west winds of the deadly moorland winters. These buildings had turfed or thatched conical roofs and in some the floor was paved.

These Bronze Age settlers had a culture which required ceremonial stone circles, menhirs (standing stones) and cists or kistvaens (burial chambers). There are known to be over 60 stone rows – single, double and triple lines of granite boulders – the biggest being the two mile stretch from Stall Moor to Green Hill, above the valley of the river Erme. Reaves, or boundary banks, can be traced in some places denoting the land of a particular family or community.

The evidence of prehistoric Dartmoor is astonishing for its wealth of antiquities and evocative names – Foale's Arrishes (Celtic fields), Trowlesworthy Warren, Kes Tor, Metheral and Drizzlecombe, Cranbrook Castle (hill fort), Holne Chase, Hembury and Hexworthy, and many, many more.

Buckfast Abbey

The only two monastic houses in Devon at the time of Domesday were the Cistercian Buckfast (c.1030) and the Benedictine abbey at Tavistock (c. 974). Endowed by Canute and affiliated to the Cistercians in 1147, Buckfast was dissolved in 1539 but revived on the original site in 1902 when the first abbot since the Reformation was elected.

Most of the buildings had been pulled down, along with a house built on the site in 1806, but it was 75 years before Benedictines returned here. A small band of devoted monks worked in all weathers to rebuild the ancient abbey. It was a 25 year *tour de force* to resurrect the abbey, where work is blended with prayer according to the old maxim of monastic life – *Ora et Labora* – Prayer and Work.

With its yellow ham-stone facing and massive tower, the style is a blend of Early English and Norman. There is a great modern east window, the work of an acknowledged stained glass craftsman, Father Charles.

Describing itself as a living monastery, the Benedictines now have a complex at Buckfast with shops selling home-made wine and honey, gifts and books and an architecturally admired restaurant. This commercial aspect is important for the maintenance of the abbey and its community as new monastic recruits decline in number.

For generations the monks have been famous not only for their sweet heady mead, a tonic wine, but also for their honey. Brother Adam, awarded an OBE for his work, and now in his nineties, has travelled the world in search of new strains of bees and his years of genetic research have produced the renowned Buckfast Bee. An apiarist's dream, this bee is not aggressive, rarely swarms, and because the hives are taken on Dartmoor in late summer, to feast on the moorland heather, they produce abundant and distinctive honey.

Tavistock

The river Tavy runs through the centre of this important market town, ten miles north of Plymouth. With a long history, it is one of the four stannary towns where people came to weigh, stamp and sell the tin from Dartmoor.

Drake was born here and the original statue of him (Plymouth's possibly more famous one, is a copy) stands looking over the canal just outside the town. Two owners really created this town. The Benedictine Abbey in the 10th century owned lands and properties stretching from Dorset to the Isles of Scilly; and the

Dukes of Bedford, who made their fortunes from the tin mines, were responsible for much of the town's development including the Gothic Guildhall and Bedford Hotel. Tin was worked in the early 1660s but then large deposits of copper were discovered. Cloth making has also played a major role in Tavistock's history and her famous weekly Pannier market was being held in the 11th century.

The author of *Brittania's Pastorals*, William Browne, was born here in 1590 and his poetry reflects his love of this beautiful area:

'My muse for lofty pitches shall not roam,
But homely pipen of my native home'

The small picture shows the originally 13th century parish church of St Eustace, which has a fine waggoned roof and carved bosses, with a Clothworker's Aisle; the exterior is made of locally mined green Hurdwick stone, popular all over the town.

In the vicarage garden is a stone, found at Buckland Monachorum, carved with strange characters called Ogham, invented in Ireland and brought over by their invaders to the west of England.

Buckland Abbey, the last Cistercian foundation, lies six miles south and is rich in associations with Drake, including the drum, which was with him when he died off Panama in 1596, and is said to beat if England is in danger.